NATIONAL GEOGRAPHIC

D0503571

# Plants on My Plate

Cathy Smith

I am eating the seeds of a plant.
These seeds are peas.

They are from a pea plant.

I am eating the leaves of a plant.
These leaves are spinach.

They are from a spinach plant.

I am eating the stems of a plant.
These stems are celery.

They are from a celery plant.

I am eating the roots of a plant.
These roots are carrots.

They are from a carrot plant.

I am eating the flower buds of a plant. These flower buds are broccoli.

They are from a broccoli plant.

flower buds

What part of a plant will you eat today?

# Index


flower buds . . . . . 10, 11
leaves . . . . . 4, 5
roots . . . . . 8, 9
seeds . . . . . 2, 3
stems . . . . . 6, 7